DEALING WITH TOUGH PEOPLE : Creative Strategies on How to Manage Difficult People in Tough Situations

RICHMOND LEE

All rights reserved. No part of this publication may be reproduced, distributed, or transmitted in any form or by any means, including photocopying, recording, or other electronic or mechanical methods, without the prior written permission of the publisher, except in the case of brief quotations embodied in critical reviews and certain other noncommercial uses permitted by copyright law.

Copyright © Richmond Lee, 2022.

Table of Contents

Chapter 1

Who is a Tough Person?

Whether it is a colleague or supervisor, a member of our family, a neighbor, a client or acquaintance... we come across tough individuals all the time. Quite simply, they're everywhere.

So knowing this to be true... wouldn't you want to discover the secret to how to get along with tough people?

Many have sought to describe or characterize what makes a person look "difficult". I believe such a list would be inconclusive... Nonetheless, a few tell-tale indications do spring to mind, such as:

- A tough person is someone who frequently lacks empathy, sympathy, or care for others. You might just say they're calloused.

- Difficult individuals tend to believe they are superior to everyone else. This sort of individual appears unapproachable while you're trying to shake their hand. They even look repulsed when you approach them as if you had some infectious sickness. Then, while chatting with them, they talk down to you as if you're lesser to them.

- Difficult individuals have aggression toward themselves. They tend to be harsh and occasionally angry toward others. This sort of trouble in a person is frequently brought on by someone who doesn't "mind their own business" and doesn't appear to have limits.

- Difficult individuals tend to be highly distrustful of others. They are quite suspicious... and many of the ideas, sentiments, and expectations they have of others are completely irrational. You may even question yourself, “Where do they come up with this line of thinking?”

- Difficult individuals have a propensity to be extremely selfish and make everything all about them.

Common Places You’ll Encounter Difficult People

Difficult neighbors

We have all had encounters with unpleasant neighbors. They generated a fuss about property lines, overgrown trees or tend to be excessively noisy in the late hours of the evening. Heck, some don’t even bother to say “hello”.

Difficult Co-workers

Bosses may frequently be challenging. With so many, the more you give... the more they desire. But bosses aren't the only tough individuals at work. Do you encounter this tough conduct from some of your employees, clients, or consumer base as well? These problematic individuals you work with appear to be working overtime at making your job harder and more stressful.

Difficult clients and customers prefer to ridicule you and even attempt to provoke you, knowing that you will lose your job if you respond.

Difficult Individuals on Social Media

Many of you have dealt with problematic individuals on your social media profiles.

For instance, you submitted a worry about something that occurred throughout your day. Next, someone who happens to be a follower or a friend of your page reads your message and feels defensive and upset with you.

This troublesome individual lives nowhere near you, and you didn't engage with them before your post to vent, but they "think "you are bad-mouthing them and attack you in the comments.

Difficult Family Members

The toughest of all unpleasant individuals to cope with every day are those inside our own families. It's not like a job where you can just find another employment because of the troubles there. It's not like dealing with problematic neighbors, where you may contemplate selling the home. It is not even like social media... where you can just block or unfriend a person and not have to deal with them anymore. With family, you just cannot always escape from the situation. Whatever your scenario may be, there are strategies to prepare yourself to better cope with challenging individuals.

Types of tough individuals

There are 4 main categories of challenging individuals. Think about the person in your life and find out the group they are in:

1. Downers; sometimes known as Negative Nancys or Debbie Downers. They constantly have something terrible to say. They grumble, criticize and judge. They are almost difficult to satisfy.

2. The better than; also known as Know It Alls, One Uppers, or Show-Offs. They prefer to attempt impressing you, name-dropping, and comparing.

3. Passives; also are known as Push-Overs, Yes Men, and Weaklings. They don't add much to discussions or people around them and allow others to do the heavy work.

4. Tanks; also are regarded as being explosive, a handful, or pushy. They want their way and would do everything to obtain it.

Chapter 2

The Improper Method to Settle a Dispute

Conventional wisdom (and research) argues that excellent communication may strengthen relationships, enhancing closeness, trust, and support. The contrary is also true: poor communication may erode ties, producing tension, distrust, and even disdain!

However, because disagreement is nearly unavoidable in relationships (and not always a sign of problems), you may eliminate a large amount of stress and develop your relationships at the same time if you have the knowledge and abilities to manage conflict healthily.

Here are some instances of bad and even harmful attitudes and communication habits that might aggravate conflict in a relationship.

Avoiding Conflict Altogether

Rather than expressing accumulating frustrations in a calm, polite manner, some individuals simply don't say anything to their spouse until they're ready to blow, and then blurt it out in an angry, cruel way. This looks to be the less unpleasant approach — avoiding a disagreement completely — but frequently causes greater stress to both parties as tensions grow, resentments fester, and a much larger dispute finally ensues.

It's far healthier to acknowledge and resolve a dispute. These assertive communication techniques will assist you to state things in a manner where you will be more likely to be heard, without being rude to the other person.

Being Defensive

Rather than addressing a partner's concerns with an objective eye and openness to comprehend the other person's point of view, defensive persons staunchly reject any wrongdoing and strive hard to avoid looking at the idea that they might be contributing to a problem.

Denying responsibility may appear to reduce stress in the short run, but generates long-term issues when partners don't feel listened to and unsolved disagreements continue to escalate.

Overgeneralizing

Overgeneralizations might raise the drama while you're settling an issue. When something occurs that they don't like, some blow it out of proportion by making sweeping generalizations. Avoid opening sentences with, "You always," and, "You never," as in, "You always come home late!" or, "You never do what I want to do!" Stop and think about whether or not this is truly true.

Also, don't bring up prior disagreements to move the debate off-topic and stir up more animosity. This stands in the way of actual conflict resolution and escalates the intensity of the conflict.

Sometimes we're not conscious of the ways the mind may inflate things out of proportion. This collection of frequent cognitive distortions may stand in the way of good interactions with people and can worsen stress levels. See which ones may be recognizable to you.

Being Right

The drive to "be right" may prolong and escalate disputes. Here's a less stressful method. It's detrimental to determine that there's a "right" way to look at things and a "wrong" way to look at things and that your method of viewing things is correct. Don't expect that your spouse views things the same way, and don't take it as a personal assault if they have a different perspective. Look for a compromise or agree to disagree, and remember that there's not always a "right" or a "wrong," and that two points of view may both be legitimate.

Psychoanalyzing/ Mind-Reading

Psychoanalyzing the other person is something to avoid in a fight. Instead of asking about their partner's thoughts and feelings, people sometimes decide that they "know" what their partners are thinking and feeling based only on faulty interpretations of their actions — and always assume it's negative! For example, deciding a late mate doesn't care enough to be on time, or that a tired partner is denying sex out of passive aggressiveness. This fosters anger and misconceptions.

It's crucial to bear in mind that we all come from a distinct viewpoint, and strive hard to assume nothing; actually, listen to the other person and allow them to explain where they are coming from.

Forgetting to Listen

Some individuals interrupt, roll their eyes, and rehearse what they're going to say next instead of listening and seeking to understand their partner. This inhibits you from seeing their point of view, and keeps your spouse from wanting to see yours! Don't overlook the significance of actually listening and empathizing with the other person! These listening abilities are vital to maintaining in mind.

Playing the Blame Game

Blaming doesn't help settle disputes. Some individuals manage disagreement by criticizing and blaming the person for the problem. They consider acknowledging any weakness on their part as a diminishing of their credibility, avoid it at all costs, and even attempt to humiliate them for being "at fault."

Instead, try to regard disagreement as a chance to study the issue objectively, assess the requirements of both sides, and come up with a solution that serves you both.

Trying to "Win" the Argument

Trying to "win" a disagreement with a loved one isn't as beneficial as trying to understand. When people are focused on "winning" the argument, the relationship loses! The point of a relationship discussion should be mutual understanding and coming to an agreement or resolution that respects everyone's needs. If you're constructing a case for how incorrect the other person is, ignoring their sentiments, and keeping entrenched in your point of view, you're oriented in the wrong way!

Making Character Attacks

Making character attacks may produce permanent harm, and isn't worth it. Sometimes individuals take any bad behavior from a spouse and build it up into a personality fault. For example, if a spouse leaves his socks lying about, looking at it as a character fault and calling him "inconsiderate and lazy," or, if a woman wants to address an issue with the relationship, labeling her "needy," "controlling," or "too demanding."

Labeling promotes bad judgments on both sides. Remember to respect the individual, even if you don't like the conduct.

Stonewalling

When one partner tries to address troublesome topics in the relationship, sometimes individuals defensively stonewall, or refuse to communicate or listen to their spouse. This demonstrates disdain and, in some instances, even contempt, while at the same time allowing the underlying dispute deepens.

Stonewalling solves nothing but produces bad emotions and ruins relationships. It's far preferable to listen and discuss things in a courteous way.

Chapter 3

Strategies for Tough Circumstances

There are going to be gloomy days. There are going to be easier and lighter periods. There is a continual ebb and flow to life and the events and experiences it throws your way.

Throughout it all, you always have an option. Do you handle the most challenging circumstances from a position of fear? Or from a place of love?

With dread, this coping may be harmful. It may be in the form of drugs, alcohol, solitude, and other harmful activities.

Or your coping might be from a place of love.

A place of love implies you are accepting compassion for yourself. It implies you may absorb the thought that 'this too will pass and remember that your identity is not the emotion you are experiencing in that time.

Because you are sad or angry does not imply you are a horrible person. Being accustomed to feeling nervous or uneasy does not indicate you are not good enough.

It is crucial to realize that you are entire and complete. Everything you need is endlessly inside you and sometimes it takes good coping skills to bring this to the surface and light.

So here are 20 healthy strategies to deal with the toughest events and emotions:

1. Close your eyes and take a deep breath in.

2. Visualize yourself on an exotic island with no problems in the world.

3. Hold an ice cube in each hand. This takes the attention off of whatever you are feeling in your mind and body.

4. Laugh out loud. Don't take yourself too seriously!

5. Listen to music you like. Start a dance party while you're at it!

6. Say this: 'Life does not offer me problems I cannot manage.'

7. Plan a vacation or something to look forward to.

8. Talk to the inner child inside. Would your inner conversation communicate to the inner child inside the way it now is? Didn't think so.

9. Close your eyes and recall eating your favorite meal or dessert as a youngster. Mmmmm delicious!

10. Remember that you were placed here to be of service. You are a vessel with a unique and powerful message to share.

11. Do five jumping jacks and get out of your way!

12. Write down everything you are scared of. Then, next to that list write down what you're doing to lessen that fear. I'm sure it's a lot more than you're aware of!

13. Clean out a closet or drawer. This brings about a sense of accomplishment.

14. Send a loving text or email. Remember that you can make a difference!

15. Go to a bookstore or online bookstore and buy yourself a book for fun and leisure.

16. Find a TV series that you can watch. When times are hard, put it on and breathe.

17. Repeat 'This too will pass.' This motto is everything. The only thing constant in life is change.

18. Write up a meal plan for yourself with healthful and nourishing foods. Look forward to accepting it and remember that it's one meal at a time.

19. Plan a routine that incorporates healthily exercising your body.

20. Light a candle or some incense. Smell the scent. Use your senses.

Chapter 4

How to Handle Disagreement Properly

A dispute is not the same as a conflict. It is a pervasive issue between two or more people that controls how they feel towards one another. There are numerous similarities in the settlement process whether you're attempting to help two coworkers or settle a dispute you have with someone. You must make an effort to meet and have frank conversations. After that, you must both listen intently and make an effort to comprehend one another's viewpoints. Finally, you should try to reach a solution that will satisfy both parties in some way.

Things to Be Aware Of

- Look for exaggerated reactions and boundary violations to confirm that you're dealing with conflict and not just a normal dispute.

- Maintain your composure, clarify everything as much as you can, and give others room to speak.

- Finding common ground and finding methods to compromise is essential when trying to settle a dispute calmly and amicably.

- When mediating a dispute, make every effort to be as equitable and fair to all parties as you can.

Techniques for Resolving Conflict

1. Pay attention to disproportionate reactions.

Conflicts aren't always the result of disagreements. Look more closely at someone's actions if they exhibit signs of distress or rage that are out of proportion to the circumstances. This can suggest that they are stressed or that they are experiencing internal turmoil. On the other hand, if their rage is directed towards another person, the two parties may need to work out their differences. In either case, you should be careful not to let this argument spiral out of control or perhaps get violent. A disproportionate reaction, for instance, would be to become upset that your friend damaged a disposable plastic cup. If a behavior or previous action has greatly offended you, consider your relationship with them.

2. Consider the tension that arises without regard to disagreements.

Whether or whether you are currently in dispute with someone, if you fight with them, you will always have animosity toward them. You might need to settle a dispute if you become irritated when they enter the room. It makes sense to try to keep your disagreement with them a secret to prevent awkward conversations. Even though a straightforward rivalry may be challenging to resolve, you should feel confident asking them for peace.

3. Consider how other people's perceptions affect your own.

Humans naturally interpret statements and deeds in the light of the speaker or the deed's personality. However, you can be at odds with them if you catch yourself casually criticizing the thoughts or efforts of others. Try to compartmentalize your relationship with them before addressing the problem so that you can evaluate their remarks and contributions objectively.
Look more closely if you notice, for instance, that a coworker creates a report that another coworker brings back for revisions. You could potentially assist them in resolving

their disagreement if they didn't take the time to attentively study the report. Their relationship is influencing how they view each other's creative output.

4. Keep your cool.

Having temper tantrums will prevent you from resolving your disputes. After all, reconciliation rather than retaliation is the main objective. Respectfully let them know that you two need to take a moment to collect yourself, using a mediator if necessary. Next, decide when and where you will talk about and settle your dispute.

Remind yourself that the objective here is to resolve the disagreement, not to prove your point, but to keep your composure. Asking them to brainstorm solutions alongside you is another strategy. This relieves some of your stress, which can enable you to unwind.

Attempting to resolve a dispute when tempers are on the rise is unsuccessful. Call a brief break if either person is agitated so that you may talk about the situation calmly.

5. List all of your worries.

Write down exactly what you believe caused the issue before you meet with the other person. As far as you can, try to ignore your personality and personal background. Consider the underlying cause of the issue and the precise changes you must make.

6. Do not interrupt the person speaking.

You can still make all your points, but be sure to give the other person a chance to voice his or her objections as well. Even if you disagree, let them finish their sentence because interjecting will just escalate the argument. It is more crucial for each of you to identify the point of contention than the "proper" resolution. The key to this approach is to work toward accepting one another's diverse viewpoints.

7. Pose inquiries

Ask the other individual a follow-up question if you don't grasp their arguments. To avoid appearing to be an interruption, be sure to wait until there is a lull in the conversation. Avoid asking harsh or sarcastic questions as they could convert the conversation into an argument. Even if you think their justifications or conclusions are absurd, keep in mind that everyone has the right to their own opinion.

A smart follow-up inquiry, for instance, could be, "When did you first discover I wasn't returning your calls?" Simply establishing a timeline for your conflict is the goal of this question.

Did you try one of the zillion other ways to contact me? is an illustration of a confrontational follow-up query. The goal of this inquiry is to make the other person feel foolish and incorrect. They'll simply become more defensive and insulted as a result, which will put you further away from finding a solution to your issue.

8. Be innovative.

Consider as many different approaches to solving the issue as you can. Before meeting, as well as while you are together and talking, you should both strive to think through the disagreement. To effectively resolve the problem, let the conversation go in as many different ways as you can, as long as feelings don't grow too heated.

You might have to let go of your preferences. For instance, the fact that your friend drove your car without your permission and almost wrecked could be the cause of your argument. They could not get why you are so unhappy about it, and as a result, your wrath has risen. If they ask first and drive responsibly, you might not mind if they use your automobile as a solution.

9. Take pauses

Feel free to take as many breaks as you both require if you feel that one of you is becoming overly emotional. As soon as voices are raised, take as much time as necessary before saying anything nasty. You could also require some time to consider their suggested line of action or solution.

10. Avoid talking negatively

Don't utter things like "can't," "don't," or "no," but rather, concentrate on the good things. The conflict will become more difficult to resolve if nasty words are used. They focus more on the problem than on the conflict. In the end, you need the other person to agree with your plan for the future.

Don't say, "I don't like the way you borrow my automobile without asking," for instance, to the other person. While this might be a crucial element of your issue, it leaves you stuck in the past during the conflict resolution process while you look for solutions. Instead, say, "If you need to borrow my automobile again in the future, we need to establish some guidelines for utilizing it." Instead of just restating the problem, this line suggests a workable remedy.

11. Find a point of agreement

There could be a disagreement that simply cannot be settled in a single conversation. Consider a resolution to the dispute that both of you can support and decide to revisit later. To effectively resolve the problem, it can need more than one conversation.
You might not concur, for instance, on the issue of whether it is reasonable for someone to take a roommate's car without

asking. But start by acknowledging that everyone was inconvenienced by the traffic incident they had with your vehicle.

12. Look for compromise

In many conflicts, no one person is completely wrong, so try to find a compromise that you can both be happy with. Always try to be the "bigger person" by finding a resolution that satisfies both of you. Don't let this turn into a competition to see who can be 'more reasonable,' however.
An example of a compromise might be giving one roommate laundry room privileges on weekend nights and weekdays, and the other on weekend days and weeknights. You can prevent future arguments over doing the laundry at the same time by switching whose turn it is to use the washing machine.

Mediating a Conflict Between Others

- Think carefully if you are the perfect mediator.

You can regard yourself as a competent counselor or a kind shoulder to cry on. However, you may not be the greatest mediator for every dispute settlement. Make sure you have a close, yet objective connection with both sides.

Family members are the finest mediators for sibling fights. Parents, elder siblings, or neighborhood friends are ideal persons to turn to for dispute resolution.

Workplace disagreements are a bit more delicate since there are rules and regulations in place to limit confrontations. Supervisors or human resource professionals are generally suitable people to handle issues. Check with your workplace handbook before serving as a formal or informal mediator.

- Get them together.

Tell the two parties you wish to assist them to work through their disagreements. Find a time they can both come together to address their dispute. They won't be able to freely share their sentiments unless they are in a room together with that aim. They may select a time themselves, or you may have to provide ideas. This will be easy if it is, for example, a workplace dispute. A supervisor can tell them that their work is suffering and they are required to discuss their conflict.

Getting two fighting friends in the same room to settle a conflict may be more tricky. The most straightforward way is to tell each of them you want to help them talk through their problems with each other. If it is too sensitive an issue, you might need to invite them to the same get-together without saying anything about the other person. This is a risky move, however.

- Take the lead

You don't need to control the entire conversation, as this may hinder organic conflict resolution. However, you might consider saying a few opening words to get them started. After all, they should know that their conflict is obvious to an impartial observer, and therefore potentially harmful. This implicit fact may bring home the reality of their conflict.

For example, you may need to explain more to children. Try telling each of them why their conflict is unhealthy and harmful. Remind them how much fun they used to have.

If you are handling a conflict between two close adult friends, you can be more brief and informal. Tell them their conflict is upsetting and uncomfortable for those around them. They need to start talking.

For workplace disputes, you may have a script or list of talking points you are legally required to cover. If not, a decent method is to inform them that their disagreement is impacting their job performance. Check with your corporate rules to determine what is required of you.

- Allow both parties to speak

The most crucial component of this procedure is offering both sides an opportunity to vent their issues. Try not to interrupt them, unless they are becoming too furious or confrontational. It is normal for them to display some emotion, as they are releasing pent-up stress.

- Listen to all sides

Keep an open mind. Even if you have a notion of who is in the right, alienating one individual by giving them less opportunity to speak won't fix the situation. You won't be able to come up with compromise solutions without listening to both sides' concerns.

- Allow for debate

After you establish the aim of the talk, you are there as an unbiased spectator. Feel free to jump in if discourse becomes heated or no one is talking. However, remember that this is a time for them to communicate, not you.

- Take a side, if appropriate

One party may be in the wrong. It may alienate one of the parties if you fail to admit that they were plainly in the right. This doesn't imply both sides aren't equally responsible for continuing the issue. However, some instances demand the frank acknowledgment that one party was more in the wrong at the base of the dispute. For example, you may opt to point out that your buddy was in the wrong for using his friend's automobile without asking.

- Offer a few sacrifices

After having heard all sides of the issue and having enabled them to speak for themselves, provide choices. Giving them alternatives makes them proactive in finding the best settlement. Offer the solutions as logical responses, not based on your opinion.

For example, you may give your buddies with automobile disagreement the following alternatives:

1. You might discontinue loaning him your automobile completely to prevent future conflicts.

2. You may continue to loan him your automobile, but make ground rules explicit.

But now you may not be able to address their situation. You don't need to come up with a solution if there is no simple answer to their dilemma. For example, if one person's partner left them for a second person, you may not have an obvious option. However, having their emotions out in the open may be helpful for both of them.

- Encourage them to make up

You should strive to convince them to complete their dispute resolution on a good note. Encourage them to inform each other that they are no longer going to keep a grudge. Pay attention to their feelings, though. Don't compel them to shake hands or kiss and makeup when they are not ready to. This may lead them from being on the road to acceptance back to wrath.

Try to avoid asking them to say they're sorry. Simply asking them to make up should prompt them to say they're sorry naturally. Saying the words I'm sorry is a matter of dispute for many individuals, and they will do it when they're ready.

Chapter 5

Getting Along With Tough People

I am sure that you have had to deal with tough individuals before but how did you get on? Dealing with tough individuals may make you modify your typical behavior, make you believe that it is your responsibility that they are acting in this manner, erode your self-confidence and badly affect your career and personal life.

Difficult individuals are prevalent in many aspects of your life. They may be challenging because they are nasty, they have to have the final word, they yell at you or raise their voices, they are always right, they undermine you, they don't listen or they do not respect their obligations. You probably will have your instances.

Here are some strategies to use while dealing with tough people:

- Accept that their actions are not personal.

Usually, the tough individual has nothing personal against you, they are simply unpleasant to everyone. Accept that you are dealing with inappropriate behaviors and work on their behaviors. Look for the person's excellent characteristics and concentrate on them.

- Act normally

When interacting with a challenging individual might make you behave differently than you typically do. You might start to avoid them or act differently towards them. Try to be yourself and treat them as you would anybody else.

- Try and comprehend them

The tough individual may be acting as such for a cause. Try to comprehend the difficult person and their point of view. They may have concerns that may be addressed which can strengthen the connection. It may be a very tiny problem that is harming them that is easily fixed.

- Communicate well

It is simple for communication to suffer with a tough individual. However, it is crucial to communicate properly with them. Try to listen to them and grasp what they are trying to say and what they desire.

- Build a friendship and trust

The tough person may be the way they are because of a lack of faith in others or others in them. Therefore spend time strengthening your friendship and confidence in each other.

- Be honest and upfront

When dealing with a tough individual be honest and upfront. If you are unsatisfied with their conduct then let them know. It is a good idea to ask them what they would want you to alter, then let them know what adjustments they may do to strengthen the connection.

- Make them feel nice

The challenging individual may suffer from poor self-confidence or self-esteem. Make them feel good about themselves by emphasizing their assets and positive attributes.

- Focus on the result

Keep focused on the result that you want to attain in your connection with the tough individual. This will assist you to stay objective and better equipped to cope with the individual.

- Find a win-win scenario

Look for a solution where both you and the difficult person gain.

- Keep your obligations and deliver

When dealing with a tough individual ensure that you respect your promises and that you deliver on what you say you will buy within the specified timeframes. This will acquire their respect and assist to create a connection with them.

- If you cannot make things work then make the choice not to deal with them.

Sometimes when dealing with a tough individual, even if you have tried many of the tactics above, you cannot make the relationship work. In this circumstance, it is typically advisable to move on and not to deal with them going ahead. Dealing with a tough individual may be highly tiring and of little worth to you. Be prepared to take a choice if need be.

When dealing with a tough individual, why not try out some of the techniques above and see if they make a difference? You will probably discover that they assist you to create a nice connection and that they are not a tough person' with you any longer.

In addition, here are 13 measures that might help you get along with tough individuals.

1. Be a good listener, particularly before responding.

Sometimes unpleasant individuals are just that way because they are going through a challenging moment in their life... and their conduct reflects that. Be the ear a person may need when they are being "hard to deal with." Try listening to them to determine the pain or frustration that the individual may be going through. You never know what is underlying their annoying conduct. Maybe they simply need to vent about it? Be the ear a person may need when they are being "hard to deal with."

2. Don't be judgemental.

Have you ever heard the adage, "When you point the finger at someone, three fingers are pointing back at you"? It is crucial when you listen to someone who tends to be tough that you do so objectively. If they are going through a hard phase in their life, you want to listen to gain perspective, not criticize them. None of us truly know how we will behave if we are in the same scenario.

3. Get someone else's viewpoint while avoiding gossip.

It is usually a wise decision to ask for another person's opinion while dealing with tough individuals. It is a chance for you to get your emotions off your chest while, at the same time, receiving an objective perspective of the problem. It is a technique of finding out "if it is them or me." Just be cautious to try to avoid obtaining the viewpoint of someone who is always agreeable... It wants to transform your talk into a gossip session.

4. Be courteous. Two wrongs don't make a right.

Don't reciprocate the conduct that you have received back to the tough individual who enraged you. Most individuals recognize that they were in the wrong and their action was excellent or terrible. Showing compassion and respect, even when it is not earned, may well be the thing that drives their heart to change.

5. Give a peace offering.

Bake a pie. Bake a cake. Give a thoughtful gift. Gifts make great peace offerings when they are well planned and thought out. Your kind gesture could be the difference-maker here, no matter how small.

6. Identify their secret need.

As you take time to listen to that problematic individual or speak the subject over with an impartial third party, you will realize that there is a hidden need that your bothersome foe has. For example, it may be that this individual has some major issue that takes them off their game... like losing a parent, having a sick kid, or going through a divorce. To cope, this individual is taking their frustration out on everyone who enters their way.

7. Offer praise

There are moments when all of us, even challenging individuals, could use some optimism in our lives. That ridged employer, colleague, or neighbor may only need to hear what it is that you enjoy or respect about them.

It might be that your boss, albeit a pain in the butt, is terrific under pressure. It might be that your colleague is incredibly tidy and organized, albeit they're hard to get along with.

Your neighbor may grate on your nerves, but they have the nicest manicured lawn and hedges in the area. Try paying them a compliment; it may go a long way. Make lemons out of lemonade, as they say.

8. Don’t demand change, but express how their behaviors make you feel.

I realize this doesn't apply to everyone. Still, while dealing with tough individuals, it is crucial to remember that difficult people are humans too. Though they are a handful, they have sentiments, and they're able to think and comprehend. So try to communicate to a difficult individual how their behaviors make you feel... and hope for the best. Maybe they will comprehend and change. It may work better than insisting someone modify their habits. That nearly always backfires.

9. Try not to take their conduct personally

Know what provokes you about their actions. Doing the best you can try not to take a difficult person’s conduct personally.

As noted previously, elements in a person's life might bring to such severe conduct. You may remark, “They know when they do this-or-that, it grates on my nerves.”

We also add, “they are doing it on purpose.” But if we give people credit for recognizing our triggers, we need to be conscious of our triggers too... and protect against the conduct that is aggravating us so intensely. Starting your day off with positive affirmations may be useful, particularly when you know you will be encountering a challenging individual.

10. Find someone who may be able to provide support.

When you have listened to a person who is being difficult because of a personal issue and recognized their need, it is crucial to inquire whether they are prepared to receive aid. If so, you should be ready to give information or a source of aid for this disturbed individual.

11. Self-reflection – Why does their conduct affect you so much?

Reflection is always a great thing. So it never hurts to think about the habits of your difficult antagonist and ask yourself, "Why is this conduct troubling me so badly?"

12. Take a careful look in the mirror; you may be the tough one everyone has a problem with

Another way to look at self-reflection is to gaze at oneself. You may discover that you are the tough one that everyone around you is struggling with. While it may be a difficult pill to chew, you notice this when you reflect and discover that everyone you contact is rubbing you the wrong way. Unfortunately, that is not an isolated incidence.

13. Distance yourself. Limit interaction.

There are situations when being pleasant with, listening to, praising, and even seeking aid for a difficult individual doesn't work. In these cases, it is important to separate yourself or minimize engagement with them as best you can. Of course, there are exceptions to the rules, even when it comes to distance and limits. But, in many instances, it can be done.

If the difficulty is at work... move departments, avoid their workstations or just be nice and eliminate any small conversation outside of what is essential to finish your daily assignment.

If on social media, ban them or erase your concern by simply "unfriending" them.

If the problem is at home, separating yourself and restricting engagement will most surely open the way for discourse.

Communication is always crucial when discussing how to get along with tough individuals, but I am aware that certain people will be difficult no matter what we do. For further information to help you get along with tough individuals, you may check this item out on wikihow.com.

Final Thoughts on How to Get Along with Difficult People

No one is arguing that you must become best friends with a difficult person... or be the one responsible for reforming them. However, there is a reason why their conduct impacts you so severely.

You may be overly sensitive. Or maybe you are the tough one, not wanting to modify your habits or opinions. Either way... now is the best opportunity to self-reflect and, if required, intervene and impact someone's life for the better.

While not all “difficult people” are awful people, we must learn to live with them and find the best we can in them. I think these instructions on how to get along with tough people will assist you along the path.

Chapter 6

Turning Hard Circumstances in Your Favor

Although we can't control precisely how much it rains, we can make a choice - let ourselves get soaked, or get out the umbrella. The rain, of course, symbolizes the tough times that we all encounter — medical diagnoses, divorce, job loss, or simply navigating the adolescent years as a parent. And, although it may not seem like it at first, something wonderful might emerge from the experience.

Researchers have noticed that sentiments of anger, melancholy, anxiety, guilt, or grief during challenging circumstances are extremely natural, and we should never strive to dismiss such feelings. But, troubles develop when we get locked in those feelings.

Receiving a severe medical diagnosis, for example, may generate psychological and physical stress – and it might even be traumatic. When patients can be resilient, they are better able to manage their medical condition, stay happy and even uncover new sides of themselves they never noticed.

There is a phrase for the process – post-traumatic recovery – and it relates to the benefit and personal progress that comes from suffering a catastrophe. Research has also indicated that up to 70 percent of individuals experience positive psychological development from tough circumstances, such as a deeper sense of self and purpose, a better appreciation for life and loved ones, and an improved capacity for compassion, empathy, and motivation to act for the greater good. While the shift from old to new was natural for the mythological creature, in the actual world we may learn how to evolve and develop no matter the hurdles we confront.

Make meaning

As we mature, we create a set of beliefs about the world around us — it's the foundation we construct our lives around. When we face terrible times, it's like an earthquake - unexpected – and it may tear up that foundation and leave us feeling uncertain of ourselves with sections of our lives reduced to rubble.

A catastrophe like a divorce or the death of a family member might raise our attention to how we take some parts of our life for granted. It challenges our very identity and beliefs we've formed leaving us to ask questions we never thought we would have to.

When we are willing to ask and explore those questions – who am I, what matters to me, what do I want my life to be about – we can begin to rebuild and construct a new foundation, often from the ground up, that is more authentic and based on who we are and what's important, rather than on the values others have placed on us. During this period of transition, it is through letting go of the ideas, roles, and components of identity that no longer serve us and having the desire to evolve into a new way of being that enables us to build our lives in a manner that feels more real and true.

Metabolize the event

Learning and learning from an event doesn't imply rejecting the emotions that come with the process. But some individuals strive to avoid bad feelings, and that may be a problem.

When we attempt to hide our sentiments, it may lead them to grow stronger in the future and hinder us from getting past the uncomfortable emotions.

It is essential that you set aside time to speak about the emotions either with a friend or a qualified expert. Give yourself time and space to experience what you're experiencing. Cry, lament or go to a solitary area outdoors and let out a primal scream of wrath. Allow the sensations to arrive, and when they do, it then becomes feasible to work through them.

Cultivate a coping strategy

One of the finest ways of processing emotions is expressive writing. Expressive writing is ideal at the times we encounter anything mild to moderate, not a terrible occurrence. It has been found to dependably benefit both psychological and physical health by lowering stress and helping us to reframe the events we're experiencing. When writing, we position ourselves in the role of the hero or heroine, not the victim, and as a consequence, it helps us to alter our viewpoint and discover new meaning in our experiences. Writing about what we've been through and the meaning we're making from the experience, allows us to make sense of our experience and often find the silver lining in the situation.

Some questions to consider while writing is:

- What do I want to be about in the midst of this difficulty?
- What would the person I want to be do right now?
- What is the gift from this experience?

Another strategy to help as we're in the midst of the experience is affirmations – short phrases we can repeat to ourselves to give us hope like, "Only good can come from this, I am safe," "Out of this current difficulty, my life will be transformed into something beautiful," "This too shall pass," or "In the end, it will be OK and if it is not

OK, it's simply not the end." And it may also help us access inner resources we may not be in touch with.

Think of a moment when you were afraid or struggled and finally, it went better than you imagined, all the hurdles you've surmounted, all the problems you've traversed, and reflect on that part of you that has gotten you through. We may rely on such instances at a later period to assist remind us that we are stronger than we believe.

It's particularly beneficial when our thinking becomes negative and there is a lot of self-doubt, anxiety, or overwhelm. Connecting back with and recalling those earlier triumphs with our inner power is stronger than any doubts or negative thoughts we may be feeling about our present difficulties.

Prioritize self-care

Self-care may help us recover. When we do something that makes us feel good in a healthy and useful manner, it might boost our mindset. And there is the bonus that frequently in times of crisis we feel helpless since there may not be much we can do. Taking care of yourself is one thing we have control over and we may feel certain we're doing our best to take care of ourselves.

One method to accomplish this is to start working towards new objectives and aspirations. Small daily action actions might offer you the feeling of purpose and progress and organization that you need. Remember to call out for additional support at this tough time, some individuals will be there for you and others who have gone through something similar can provide their viewpoint and encouragement. And if you find yourself stuck and suffering, don't hesitate to seek out your physician for professional support if required.

www.ingramcontent.com/pod-product-compliance
Lightning Source LLC
LaVergne TN
LVHW050341160826
845677LV00014B/3736

* 9 7 9 8 3 5 3 0 9 9 9 6 3 *